Jennie Farley

HEX

Indigo Dreams Publishing

First Edition: HEX
First published in Great Britain in 2018 by:
Indigo Dreams Publishing
24, Forest Houses
Cookworthy Moor
Halwill
Beaworthy
Devon
EX21 5UU

www.indigodreams.co.uk

Jennie Farley has asserted her right under the Copyright, Designs and Patents Act 1988 to be identified as the author of this work.

ISBN 978-1-910834-87-9

British Library Cataloguing in Publication Data. A CIP record for this book can be obtained from the British Library.

Designed and typeset in Palatino Linotype by Indigo Dreams.
Cover design by Ronnie Goodyer.
Printed and bound in Great Britain by 4edge Ltd.

Papers used by Indigo Dreams are recyclable products made from wood grown in sustainable forests following the guidance of the Forest Stewardship Council.

For my goddaughter, Louise Monaghan, with love

Acknowledgements

Grateful acknowledgment to those editors of magazines and webzines in which some of these poems first appeared: *Prole, Lunar Poetry, Artemis, Broadsheet, Amaryllis, Atrium, Clear Poetry, Mslexia, The Cannon's Mouth, Three Drops from a Cauldron.* My thanks also for invitations to share my poetry at readings: Anna Saunders, Director of *Cheltenham Poetry Festival;* Miki Byrne *In Your Own Words Poetry Group;* Sharon Larkin & Roger Turner *Poetry Cafe – Refreshed,* Rebecca Sillence *Cheltenham Library Pop-Up Poetry Cafe,* and to my many poetry friends who have supported me. A special thank you, as always, to David Clarke for his continual encouragement, advice, and help with my writing; and to Hannah Keeling for her perceptive and sensitive reading of the poems. Finally, heartfelt gratitude goes to my publishers, Ronnie Goodyer and Dawn Bauling of Indigo Dreams Publishing, for having faith in my work.

Also by Jennie Farley:

My Grandmother Skating (IDP, 2016)
Jocasta's Song (Griffin Press, 2015)
Masks and Feather (The Palms Studio, Cornwall, 2012)

CONTENTS

HEX

She was feeling supernatural tonight,
she wanted to eat diamonds
Angela Carter, Nights at the Circus

Changes

This is how things change.
When you step outside a bar
into a glistening street of neon pink
where a man with a moustache is waiting
beneath a lamp with a bunch of lilies.

When you notice that bones
are being worn outside the skin
like gloves, when the scar on your ankle
has become a tattoo of a small curved dagger,
when the autumn bushes in your garden
are a rage of tigers, and rotting geraniums
ooze menstrual blood.

When your pet cat turns feral, all
snarling and claws, and the cushions
in your sitting-room look furious.
When you see the town pigeons
stamping out a code on the pavements,
when one hundred seagulls rise and swoop
in formation over Sainsbury's.

When you sleep in the afternoon
and your dreams take you to another,
yet familiar, place, when at night every face
in the universe shows itself to you one by one.

When conversation becomes silver sound
like a symphony heard but not understood,
when a glass-bottomed boat upturns
and the sky is full of fish.

Lynx

I met my friend reborn as a lynx,
slinking around the bins at the back
of my house. I recognised
her cat-green eyes. She was wearing
my tears as a string of pearls.

We went off into the forest,
a shawl of frost hugging my shoulders.
We left our prints in sudden snow.
I hadn't locked my door.
I knew I would never return.

Looking up at an indigo sky
I saw the outline of a lynx
like a sketch by Galileo.
The silver charm she'd given me
dropped from my throat.

We will follow our spirit guide,
leaping galaxies on claw-studded paws,
scattering the dust of all those secrets
of love and betrayal we shared, curled
up on her black velvet sofa.

On planet earth we are wrapped in fur,
striped with colours of fire and ice.
Our black-tufted ears stand alert
for the call of wild to wild.

The reach of the universe is ours –
but we'll stay true to our animal spirit,
playing among trees and rocks,
living our afterlife with grace.

Magdalen of the Valleys

Behind the gold mask is the skull of the Magdalen,
jewels glitter in the sockets of her eyes.
The red-wattled cockerel chuckles at the sun.

She was the watcher in the shadow of the Cross,
neither whore nor mother, yet wracked with His pain.
Through the garden of sorrows to the empty tomb,

she was witness to the stench of bloodied cloth,
aloes, vinegar. Desert crows wait in vain for carrion.
The clay pot of Gospels is buried deep in sand.

She is the woman drawing water from the well,
grief running bloodless through her veins,
the voice of the Valleys keening in her bones,

harp-song plucking at her wounds.
The red-wattled cockerel crowing.

The Summons

This morning he awoke as from some dark dream
he couldn't quite recall, a thrumming in his mortal
blood. *Come to me tonight when the moon is high.*

Heat-baked paths ridged by chariot wheels, wooded
folds, the Sacred Grove garlanded with steaming pelts
and strewn with bones, an ivied portal opening

onto moon-glazed shore. At the sea's
edge he waits for her, foam curdling around
his sandaled feet, his heart drumming.

Then over by the rocks a swirl of water, a dark glitter ...
tall, robed in fish-scales, her voice rough and low
like the ocean's pull. *My son!*

*

Bathed in her absence he feels more god
than man. He traces the travel of her fingertips -
his brow, his mouth, his throat, the trail of fine hair

from chest to belly. He rests his hand between
his thighs. A sadness, a shadow-memory of
that other water, blackness rank with dead things,

her relentless grasp, his fear of falling. He turns
from the empty sea, recovers his scattered garments,
limps homeward to the palace, his ankle throbbing.

Blodeuwedd

They went into the woods to gather
flowers for my wedding, meadowsweet,
broom, flowers of the oak, weaving
a circlet to place on my head, but the petals
prickled, the thorns tore my veil.

She is made for him, his mother boasted.
How my bridesmaids envied me!
He was handsome enough in his officer's
uniform, but his eyes were cold,
his lips touching mine tasted of frost.

I wanted a lover full of fire.
I went into the woods alone at twilight,
walking the white flower path of my myth.
I found him beside the great oak, sweat-stained,
whistling to himself as he fashioned a spear.

What we did was wrong. Every night I lie
alone in my marriage bed trying not to think
of all that blood. But I can't help hearing
wings beating at the window, the scratch
of claws scraping the glass with my name.

Sacrifice

A harbour breeze flutters my skirt,
tickle-kisses limbs that feel so strange.
How I miss the languish of blubber,

the thump and flip of fin. I loiter at
the docks, waiting for his ship, for him,
the man I saw leaning on the prow.

I swam up close, arching my neck,
my silvery hair rippling down my back,
my breasts rising above the foam. He smiled,

and I was caught as in a trawler's net.
I paid the price with my severed tongue,
the waves awash with the blood of my lost

voice as I took the foul paste the sea-witch
fed me. My new legs are two spikes. At each
step I take I tread on blades. But when I think

of him, I feel a quickening at the tender fold
where my legs join, though meshed in pain. I ache
for him. But I know our passion will be a sword.

Salome

I wanted no one else but you.
Did you think me too young, or plain –
too forward? Or were you just too holy?

All men want me. Look at that fat one
sprawling on his throne, bloated like a pig,
his birds-nest crown toppling into his wine.

My mother, pissed again, hisses in his ear.
I let the silks at my waist slip a little,
let my thighs loll, lick my lips to a pout.

Anything is yours if you will dance for me.
My bare feet slap on marble, my breasts bounce,
my skirts become a frenzied whirl of fire

as the musicians madden to crescendo.
What power I have. *Anything you want.*
Your bleeding head is brought me on a plate.

My eyes feast upon the gore at your gaping mouth.

None of her Doing

In her heart she is still,
the storm's eye.

Yet here is disorder.
Books, pictures, plates
displace themselves, doors slam,
lights come on, unaccountably.

Everyone picks on her.
They unravel her, make wooden
her gossamers. Can't they see
she is rare, like a Kashmiri shawl
that can be drawn through a wedding ring.

Here the din and the dancing
shatter the fragile globe she holds
in her hands, her spinning world,
splinters reassembling as frozen laughter,
a chrysalis of herself, each icy star-particle
pulsing through space.

The cloven hoof, the disturbances, all this
has nothing whatsoever to do with her.

Stolen Fruit

Blackberries, apricots, apples and pears,
greengages, mulberries, black cherries, plums.
We flee from the market, our pinafores full,
through the glen to the brook where kingcups grow.

We splash in the shallows, sprinkle our hair,
make chains of flowers bright as the sun.
Giggling, we feed each other stolen fare.
Away with the fairies, Mother would say.

We lie down together, my sister and I.
Our kisses taste of damsons rich as blood,
peaches sweet as country wine,
quince juice, tart as our Mother's tongue.

Sated, into the dark we go, through tunnels
of rat-crawl, bat-dust, hung with shrouds,
heaped with bones of ivory and gilded skulls,
a silver penny hanging like a crookéd moon.

I waken to a chill wind, morning dew,
my arms unloosed and my sister gone.
Alone, I weep for my stolen days,
wrapped in a web of her ashen hair.

Snow

They put me in my old wool coat,
tugging and pulling, fingers prodding.
They try to brush my hair. Feathers
from the beaten quilt fly like gossip
around the wimpled heads. *Time for your walk.*
Outside it's snowing. In my head I hear
the layering of sounds, birdsong, chanting,
the sanctus bell, the distant voices of lost saints.
They give me medicine. The world is muffled.
My mouth is thick with cloth. My leaden footsteps
take me on my daily penance, self-imposed. Along
the cedar walk the trees close in, the gravel path is hard
with frost. Icy cobwebs lace my mittened hands.
I must touch the trunk of each and every tree,
genuflecting as I go. *Now and for evermore shall be so.*
At a black-ivied bell tower is a hidden corner,
broken statues, rotting leaves, a rusting pram,
a small grave strewn with long dead flowers.
This grave is mine. I lie down on the whitening mound.
I close my eyes, open wide my arms, my sleeves
outspread like wings unfurled. I rock from side to side.
I hear sad cadences of half-remembered hymns.

I crawl to my knees, mouth a silent prayer,
and turning see the imprint of an angel,
a scattering of petals crystallised.
The pockets of my old coat are filled
with blessings, my bowed head
veiled with falling snow.

Shadows

The man who stands in the curtained shadow
doesn't hold out his hands to me as others do
with flowers, gifts, unwanted platitudes.
He never could. Not since that day
when the world tipped over and emptiness
rang in our ears. I say *our* for I know
his held-in suffering matches mine.

In bed we lie apart, our words
come out all wrong, touch means
nothing. We are like shy young lovers
afraid of corrupting something precious.

One night in a kind of desperation
we clutch each other, thrusting
through pain to a place where
we've never been, blood-dark and raw.

Afterwards shrouded in shame
for our mutual forgetting, we return
to our separate shadows, remain there,
waiting for the urgent baby cry that never comes.

Ashes

If they'd given me ashes
I would've come to the river,
and let the gentle water carry him
downstream, on a prayer –

but here I stand, empty-handed,
imagining tiny fin-like limbs flailing
against the dispassionate flow

of the estuary taking him away
from me, and out to the cold
unreachable sea.

October

I shouldn't feel like this.
Almost happy. Letting
the autumn sparkle
take me to where
the trees seem
to be dancing.

Where mums
with carry-cots
smile at small boys
bashing conkers,
where the Sunday band
is playing for the last time
this year.

My life loosens
against a drift of sorrow,
a plague of endorphins
rises on the still warm air.

Colouring In

Sitting in the kitchen to avoid
messing the neat front room,

he lays his chalks out in a row.
At play school they are told

to colour in rabbits, a cottage,
a pot of flowers. But he likes

the pictures in the *Ladies' Journal*,
ladies who look just like her.

Finger-waved hair, red lips, silk floaty gowns.
He loves her pale-pink powdery smell.

*

Sitting beside the coffin in a strange, cold room,
curtains drawn, a single lamp turned low,

he holds a small embroidered bag.
Inside a box of Coty, swansdown puff,

a pot of rouge. He gently strokes
her wisping hair, dusts her cheeks,

colours her bloodless lips with pink

Pearls

They met at a tea dance, perfectly matched.
My mother with newly bobbed hair, my father
debonair in grey flannels. In snapshots
they are always turned to each other.
The day he died, she wept, *Who will
be here now to fasten my pearls?*
On this anniversary I watch my mother,
a frail form in her old winter coat, buffeted
by sleet as she searches for the tree
we planted in his memory. Suddenly
she turns to me, smiles, holds out her hand.
She is a girl again. And to some ballroom music
only she can hear, we are dancing together,
waltzing, in and out of the willows.

Vanilla Slices

I wouldn't say no to a vanilla slice,
says my mother in a plaintive voice.
She is only a ghost so I leave her
sitting on the sofa by the fire,
put on my coat, and go up to the Co-op.
Returning, I put my shopping on the table,
two vanilla slices, and a bottle of vermouth.
Whoopee! cries Mum, waving
her legs in the air. She's turned
into a flapper with newly bobbed hair.
I sit down beside her, flipping
my georgette skirt, raise my
glass in a toast to us both.
Tomorrow we'll go shopping!

Jocasta's Song

Let's say fate was to blame.
He was lifted from the birthing
sheet and placed in my arms.
I watched him grow beautiful.

I fed him, soothed him when he cried,
kissed his grazed knees when he fell.
They took him away to the mountains.
I wept.

Years passed. That fair young Prince,
the King of Thebes, was offered me
to be his wife. The Oracle's prophecy
meant nothing to me.

Many men sleep with their mothers
in their dreams. Those strong hands,
that sleepy look when he held my breasts,
his mouth. This is not the story of the phallus

but the womb, the mother reclaimed
from the empty curse laid upon her son.

The Constant Loom
Penelope

I weave the stretch of cloth and draw
It tight, ready to unpick and start again
My thumb snags on a pin. The pale threads
turn to red and I am pricked to rage.

I recall our wedding night when I oiled
your shoulders, finger-dried your hair,
joined you in our bed. O fickle husband!
sweet-talking your way into every woman's

heart while I, your constant wife, straddle
my loom keeping my vow. Twenty years
you keep travelling, while I hold off with
false promises suitors swarming at the gates.

The one with the scorching smile,
the one with swivelling hips, the sweet boy
with a voice seductive as harp song. I could've
had them all. My maidservants did to their great cost.

Now it's time to revoke my vow. This shroud will be
completed soon, my thread-raw fingers racing skeins
across the spools, the pooling fabric telling a lament for
my lost years, and for the twitching feet of the hanged maids.

Playing
Circe and Odysseus

I would play at turning men into beasts –
wolves, mountain lions, wild pigs.
Because I could. I gave them drugs
to keep them quiet. I watched them
prowl and weave among my rich
hangings, gilded chairs, rubbing
against my skirts, waiting to be petted.

He came with his crew
to my island house of stone.
I changed his men into swine
so I could have him all to myself.
I fed him chicken baked in herbs,
barley cakes, figs and lotus fruit and wine.
I bathed him in waters from my cauldron,
anointed his body with oils of neroli and rose.

He lay with me in sheets of scented linen,
caressed me with his hands and tongue –
he wanted to stay with me for ever.
I wanted to play with him,
that's all. It was everything.

Hera
Wife of Zeus

For eighteen years I polished his helmet,
sewed on gold braid, served him oysters
cooked in cream, artichokes, figs,
and strong sweet wine. Of course,
I knew about his child.
Every night I lay submissive
by his side, plotting my revenge.

It'll be easy. I will approach this
tender boy who's not yet set in hardness.
He'll be leaning on the bridge where
oleanders sweep down to the bank,
pulling on a roll-up. He will go with me.

Lying sleek in his unknowing arms
among the warm sweet river smell,
it will be pleasure that consumes me.
Afterwards, as I lick the sweat
from his smooth throat, I will smile
into my husband's eyes.

Hyppolyta, Queen of the Amazons

I sliced off my right breast with my sword,
the better to steady the bow, and draw
the arrow straight across the chest.

I swore to forego motherhood and sex,
so try to shrug off the shadow-memory
of a baby's milky breath, the touch

of a lover's bearded lips. Now I braid my hair
into a helmet, wear a breastplate of leather,
bronze bangles, a necklace of the enemy's teeth.

Like my scar, I wear with pride my sacred Girdle,
the War-God's gift, as I lead my women into
battle, urging our lathered horses onward .

We've learned how to slay, unflinching, with sword
and spear. Although vengeful killing is never our
main intent. This is just to show men that we can.

If I Could

If I could reach the wolf of you,
beyond the sleek lover, the human truth,
down deep through caves of foetid sloop
to the whimpers, the fur, the musk of you,
as lost to our world you suck on dreams.

In feral dark I would lie with you,
adorn your mane with a diamond sheen.
I would lick your paws, anoint your pelt
with my woman's scent, feed you
apples of the moon.

Like Glass

When I feel myself unravel
I think of you, how you take my hand
and place it where it wants to be,
your clever hands weaving me
into a garment of light.

Outside the window
the afternoon belongs to other people
as we turn day into night where
everything is possible, like taking
a piano into the garden or dancing
in an empty room beneath a chandelier.

Then I must let the memory go
before I feel myself break, like glass.

Once

I loved you once. When afternoons
were hot and blue, and cool woods
led us to our place.

I loved you once. My heart sparked
by a gesture or a glance, our eyes
locked in sweet conspiracy.

I know that love can't last, that it will
alter just as stormclouds ride the sky,
and sailboats leave the harbour for the sea.

I loved you. And now that you are gone,
I wear our bruised love like a badge
to match the faded bloodstrings of our vow,

remembering how we could cause the stars
to dance. O how I miss the dazzle and the bright!

The Gift
after Paula Rego

She remembers as a child painting
          the strangeness of things –

a cabbage with crenellated leaves
          the size of a castle,

the skull-head of a horse
          roaring out prophecies,

Gentleman Dog strumming on a mandolin.

She weaves the smoke of dreams from
          the clay pipe between her lips.

See how the lion crouches above
          the shawled head of her muse.

Sofia

Her feet are bare.
Brazilian hoops furnish her ears

veiled by a heavy sweep of hair.
She wears silk skirts patterned

in the red and black of remembered pain,
she shows defiance by a slipping shawl.

Accepting her new reality, she displays
with pride the stretched scar where

her left breast once was. Like those
self-maimed warrior women riding

into battle with triumphant songs,
she challenges us with a burnished stare.

Reverence

A screech of tyres on tarmac.
The wet gleam and slippery stain.
He takes the still warm fox
into his arms, cradles it,
watching the eyes glaze
as something like a soul
passes into the wherever.

At home with his camera
he holds the weight of fur
against his bare white skin,
embracing his own fear.
The shutter clicks.

Then comes dreamtime.
Days spent in the darkroom
with its arcane smell,
the wonder of seeing images
evolve in dim amber glow.
Getting everything right –
every claw, every whisker, every hair.

Stone Child, Bone Child

I was twelve years old, my skirt
tucked up, paddling in the rock pools.
Collecting pebbles, shells. Then I saw it
among the bladderwrack, a shining.
They came from the town with spades,

found more bones – skull, ribcage,
a splattered tail. The whole measured
twelve feet long. They said it was a miracle.
In the beginning was the Word,
and the word was *ichthyosaurus*.

From then on every moment
I spent down at the bay, chipping
at the tideline, picking through
time's archives. They came from
far and wide to view my findings.

I have no book-learning, but I've
argued with clever men and been
proved right. I've had no time
for friends or family. There was
a man once, but nothing came of it.

At the foot of the road to the sea
is a small museum named in my honour.
These labelled specimens will last for ever
to be marvelled at. But I am old now,
and too tired to deal with miracles.

Miss Havisham Goes Shopping

She reaches for the jewellery stand,
the dangling beads roped like her
wrists, her blue-veined hands.

She fondles them. She wore the real
thing once. Age spots show through
threads of hair wisping like the cobwebs

in that shadowed room among the tulles
and nets of the faded wedding dress.
She doesn't know this man

in the black broad-shouldered coat
wheeling her along the Arcade and into
Debenhams. She doesn't know herself.

Cardy, trimmed slippers, a rug of crocheted
squares over her knees. These clothes
were never hers. Memories mist her mind.

A looking glass. A veil of lace. At her throat
a string of pearls glistening like tears.
All those years she waited for him.

He never came. She watched time guttering
away as candles on the frosted cake
dissolved in pools of wax.

Black Cherries

I hate this dress, the lace scratches,
the satin bow's too tight.
I hate the locket dangling

on my chest with Grandmama's
dead hair. These pointy-toed satin
slippers nip my toes. *I hate pink!*

I hate Mama, I hate Marietta
and her horrid hand-me-downs,
I hate Nurse, her slaps and pinches.

But most of all I hate *him*, his beady eyes
probing as he paints, his fingers creeping
down my throat as he adjusts

my collar. He has me lick a cherry
picked from the goblet on the table,
then takes up his brush. The floor

seems to slip and shudder, candles
flicker sideways, my thoughts go black.
Tomorrow I will get up early, choose

a cherry from the goblet, go to
the pantry and dip it in Nurse's
tin of rat-kill. I will pose sweetly

in my dress of prickly *marquisette.*
When he's laid the final brushstroke
he will approach me, leering,

and I will smile, take the cherry,
tempt his bearded lips. The bitterness
of the fruit. Its stony heart.

Vintage

Dinner, and he's floundering like a drowning fly.
The wife's parents, and Mr and Mrs *Whatsaname*
who've just moved in next door.

Impatience slinks around his neck.
He makes a point of glancing at his watch.
The dog jumps up, wags its tail.

From the kitchen he takes the wife's
Saturday-job key from its hook, his mac, torch.
A brisk walk, one turn of the key, and he's in

the midnight shop he calls Rosinaland, where
torchlit spangles twinkle, satins slide and shift.
Rosina awaits him in her scarlet gown,

blonde wig and bowler hat. Off with his mac,
outdoor shoes, trousers, golf jumper, socks.
On with the gown, the wig, the hat.

A slick of *Coral Kiss*. On with the heels.
The backlit mirror flaunts his catwalk twirl,
a tip of the hat ... The dog yawns.

1926

What do they know
of the ecstasy beating
beneath my black sealskin coat?

I remember the satin sheen
of those Italian nights
awash with wine and violins,

the peacock cries,
the sleek-backed striding dogs
dangerous as thoughts.

That woman in the silver cloche was me.
We danced, and then you walked away.
Now love has made me greedy.

Love has made me patient.
Warm as a fertile egg, my heart
waits for your sign. In the Piazza

as you salute the crowd, I will hold
your gaze, then dive into my purse,
savour the touch of metal. The gun.

I Knitted You a Halo

The light's not good, but I will do my best.
The pigeons and the damp are to blame.
Every morning I sweep up their mess
and heaps of crumbled plaster
from your poor ruined face.

But it was never a good likeness.
I should know, you're my dear friend.
Remember when we broke bread together
over a bowl of homemade soup.
I washed your feet, patted them dry
with rose-scented talcum.
I knitted you a halo, but you said, *No!*
You were never one for showing off,
except that time you walked on water.
I tried it once, the boating lake.
People laughed as they hauled me out.

I wear a neat hat, a pinafore,
sensible shoes. I take pride in polishing
the pews, arranging the hymnals just so,
lighting candles, watering the Easter lilies.

No one knows I'm up here with my box
of paints, but soon my work will be done.
On Sunday when I kneel before the altar
to sip your blood, take your body
in my mouth, I will nod a smile at the wall
where your new face glows. And feel blessed.

The Zoo-Keeper's Daughter

Your baby sister's crying.
Well, she'll feel better
when she's grown some fur.

The room is full of milkbreath,
camphor. Creatures.

In the early light I see
a giant mouse, an Abyssinian baboon
bubbling rainbow colours,
and a snowy-faced llama.

Look out! That marmoset
is about to bite. O holy thumb!
O greedy stars! O monkey arms!

Clap hands if you believe in crocodiles!

Something slithers beneath the bed.
Tell me it's only a dream,
I know other.
The whiff of sulphur,
the curled feather drifting,
the claw-mark on my wrist.

Boarding the Bus as a Wolf

She leaps the step, pays her fare
with silver claws. Golden eyes

gleam through thick kohl slits.
She sinks into a vacant seat.

Layered in ragged furs, grey,
white-tipped, matted wet

from forest earth, yet she appears
reposed and calm as she holds

the rough skins tight around her.
The evening bus is full. Chattering,

breathing each others' warmth,
the passengers seem unaware

of the figure shawled in winter dark
crouched amongst them. The bus draws

to a halt. Wolf ears twitch, and with one bound
she is off, skittering on horn-shod feet through

the Christmas crowds, a drawn-out howl
soaring above the carol singers' chorus.

Cannibal Stew

My missionary great-uncle found
a severed toe in his hot-pot, and
not wishing to offend the tribal chief,
or displease God, he swallowed it.
He was never quite the same again.

He seemed to himself altogether jollier,
almost raunchy, you might say.
He removed his polished boots
to feel the hot thud of bare sand
as he pirouetted in the sway
of his cassock (his own tribal dance).
He was aware of the kohl-black eyes
of the chieftain's fifteen wives, their
large bright-feathered swaying rumps,
noted in his journal how many times
each day he experienced a penile erection.

Back home in Peckham he thought
how well jungle drums enlivened
Morning Prayer, how the Communion
wine benefited from a dash of rum.
At Parish dinners he was life and soul
with his ribald stories, although
he always avoided anything resembling
a meat casserole. He suffered
problems with his dentures.

The Day I Rescued a Merman

I found him washed up on the beach
slumped against the coastguard station.
His face was beautiful like the carving of a god,

his chest bronzed though streaked with salt.
I sat down beside him and gently stroked
his tail. It wasn't slithery, but warm and dry,

the scales glittering like his sea-glass eyes.
I took him home for a fish supper. We slouched
on the sofa, licking our fingers. I'd hoped for

tales of buried ship treasure, mermaids, whales,
but he didn't speak, just smiled. I ran him a bath,
testing for sea chill with my elbow. He slid down

in the water, folded his tail over the side,
closed his eyes. I like to think he found pleasure
in the scented bubbles, in the love songs I crooned to him.

Silk Scarf and Tambourine

I knew one day I would run away
and join the circus, ever since
I was given a bright silk scarf
and a tambourine by my wayward uncle.

That day I mounted a piebald pony
shaking a bridle of tiny tinkling bells
and tassels as it trotted along the High Street,
away from the town of everyday.

Inside, the tent was all a-spangle, there
were smells of horse dung and straw,
and something old and powdery and secret.
High up astride a silver crescent moon

a girl with painted skin and cowboy boots
rocked herself, her lips moving to some
hillbilly music playing in her head.
I wanted this crazy girl to be my friend.

This crazy girl took up her needle, drew all
over my back tendrils and curlicues in circus
colours. Bare-breasted we rode a bare-back stallion
as the ringmaster, my wayward uncle, cracked his whip.

Knives

You feel in control throwing knives at your Mum.
I'm practising my act, while she stands statue-still

her back against the wagon. The sharp blades
send chips of red paint flying around her.

No one's about except the juggler twins rolling
in the dust with their black-and-tan cur.

Everyone's sprawled and snoring in their bunks,
an afternoon snooze until the ringmaster cracks the whip.

I'm thinking of all those shenanigans with Mum,
the Royal Crown Derby smashed to smithereens,

the screaming, the curses. *You wicked girl!*
An inch to the right, and I'd slice off

an earring, rip the fringe of the crimson
shawl. Or I could aim for the bull's eye –

the exact spot on her forehead
between the eyes.

Skin

I inked your name upon my knee
when I was practising my art,
my ring of needles circling
the pain one must expect from
love etched on bone. Love unrequited.

One day you'll come into my parlour
to pay for my perfected art. I will start
with the hot scratch of a tiger's claw
sinking into collarbone. Skulls, daggers
and chrysanthemums, an eagle's
spread, a chain of feathers.
It will take some time.

My gloved fingers
will work slowly, following
the serpent's trail scaling
your back. My hurting love
scrawled all over your skin,
my name spiking your heart.

Hex

How did they work it, this dark magic,
our forbears who painted cave walls,
with mammoth, bison, speared
for happy hunting, necromancers
holding worded spells over flame,
mumbling witches stirring a broth of herbs.

Me, I took up my felt-tipped pen, sketched
her face on the back of my note book,
coloured it in to look like Warhol's
portrait of Marilyn, my fingers poised
with the tip of a sharp and rusty pin.

Picking Rosemary

I could be a sorceress as I cut
the twiny stems and release a smoky
scent like burning herbs, memories
fusty as a swarm of bats.

The smell of scorched milk in the kitchen,
burnt toast, while Mum and Dad squabble.
The baccy breath of Granddad bouncing
me on his rough tweed knee.

Winter sniffles, chapped lips, chilblains,
the whiff of Vicks Vaporub and ZamBuk.
Loitering on my way to school through
the acrid scuffle of crackling leaves.

Our special hiding-place in bracken,
damply warm. Sharing a roll-up
behind the wall. The first real kiss,
tongues tasting of peppermint.

That day when I *started*.
Stomach ache, stained knickers,
a rusty tang It was Sunday lunchtime,
the Easter joint of lamb steaming on the plate.

Blood Brothers

I used to be Robin Hood
roaming the forest behind
our house, carving *Robin* into

the bark of trees. Not Maid Marian,
too mumsy with her cambric skirts
and flaxen braids. The thigh-length

boots appealed to me. I cropped
my hair, collected long green feathers,
my Granddad taught me archery.

Hold tight the bow, and let the arrow fly.
The gymslip girls were my Merry Men.
They followed me through waist-high bracken,

braving sticky green spears to the fence
where the ferrets were nailed. We dared
each other to touch the feet. We smeared

our bloodied fingers across each other's
cheeks. Blood brothers now, we plundered
the woods for willow and yew, gathered

whortleberries, wild sorrel and nuts
which we fed each other in earthy dark,
as we hid from the Sheriff in the mighty oak.

Skinny Dipping

You should go skinny dipping, he says.
It will free you up. I fling off
my evening dress, and jump.
I never thought the Cherwell
could be so cold in May.

The icy splash embraces me.
Hands of frosted ice stroke my arms,
thighs, breasts. My lips tingle
with astonishment. I never thought
it would feel so good, a delicious pain,
a *coup de foudre.* I feel free (he is right
about that), but not freed up to let him
chortle filthy words in my ear, shove
his fat tongue into my mouth,
grab my bottom with a big hot paw.
Next year he can take someone
else to the Ball!

I am free and floating. In love
with myself. I am wearing water
like a silk gown, a lover's gift.

I swim away from the river bank, away.

The Clasp

Is she human, that one?
Those brawny blokes
with inked forearms
and bruised knuckles
can't look her in the eye,
that lass with purple hair.
She's felled Big Mack
in two minutes flat.
No one offers her a drink.

Then he strides in, a stranger.
Gives a wink, pulls out a chair,
rolls up his sleeves. She crosses
black skull-patterned legs, offers
up her rubbed-raw elbow. He places
his thumb around her grip.

Then there's this moment.
She meets his hard blue gaze.
She can sense his muscled arm,
she wants to lick the raised
blue vein throbbing in his neck.
*Roll that wrist, pull backwards,
close in*, she tells herself.

She lets her elbow slip.

Grandma Jenkins

Grandma Jenkins stirs her porridge
the wrong way. She doesn't feel

the need for teeth. Her eyes
are sharp as tin. On warm days

she sits at the cottage door, her skirt
stretched wide, shelling peas.

I hurry past on my way to school,
but can't resist a backward glance.

Would she put a spell on me?

Once I dared myself to stop
and say, *Good morning!*

Grandma Jenkins beckoned me
close, I could smell her baccy breath,

she leaned forward with a cackle,
chucked me under the chin. I ran

and ran. I haven't yet turned into a rat
or an owl, but I go to school another way.

Tea Candles

There was this woman – let's call her
Maud – who went about helping herself
to things in shops. She was the kind
of person should keep a cat, eyes the blue
of a child speechless with joy at a birthday party.
She wore a flowered frock with lots of smocking.
She left her large shopping trolley in the hall.

Her front room was a tottering tower
of glorious booty, jewelled slippers,
velvet gowns, fur capes, things
she'd never wear.

There was a drawer full of tea candles,
a small table laid with lace doilies,
fairy cakes, sherry in tiny glasses
to welcome visitors who never came –

and no one would ever see inside
the airing cupboard on the landing,
each shelf heaped with bootees,
knitted baby bonnets, plastic
rattles of pink and blue.

The Summerhouse

She's ready for a sit-down. Someone has put
out a deckchair. She sits, and looks around.
Someone's pruned the roses, but it isn't
Keith's day, at least she doesn't think so.

Billy's left his scooter out. Whatever
would a bank manager want with a scooter?
She could do with a cuppa. She can smell rain.
She heaves herself to her feet, sets off up the garden.

Someone's moved the summerhouse. How did
that happen, she'd only been gone five minutes
to the post-box. A person she doesn't recognise,
with a key is trying to get into her house.

In the Attic

She would dance in the attic
in the middle of the night,

jigging to some old tune
playing in her head,

on the floor tin soldiers,
broken dolls, a jigsaw

with pieces of blue sky missing.
When they come searching,

as in time they will,
the attic is the last place

they'll think to look.
They will tramp up the stairs

calling her name, wave a torch
at the mouth of the open trap –

where wafting cobwebs will part
to reveal a humming dance
of silvery wings.

Meeting Jesus on the Beach

You followed me along the beach.
As you strode past, your bare feet

kicking up the sand, you thrust
some papers into my hand.

The Holy Gospels. That was
how I knew it must be you.

Now I am following you.
Some might call it stalking.

I see you at all the spots
where summer tourists gather,

pushing your pamphlets at everyone
who passes. Later at the beach bar

I watch you drinking with a bunch of lads,
joining in their banter. Boys' names

are tattooed with arrowed hearts along
your forearm. *Matthew, Mark, Luke, John.*

Your head gleams like a halo in the sun.
Everyone wants to take your picture.

To say I am in love with you would be
profane. All I'm wanting is your smile.

Lost

The point of a maze is getting lost.
says my geeky brother.
You can always work it out.

The hedges smell of old summers,
or funerals when the coffin passes
through the lych gate. I can't see

over the tops even if I stand
on tiptoe. The winding paths
all look the same, I no longer hear

Mum calling. I shiver in my thin
summer frock as the sky grows
cold. Everywhere becomes lost

in winter dark. Turning a corner,
I follow a long-robed figure
leading the way, candle in hand.

Is this where all the lost Souls go?
The hedges are frost-silvered, a tracery
of twigs form a glittering cage.

Inside is a girl who looks like me.
She is sitting cross-legged, her pale fingers
strumming on a dulcimer.

Playing Catch

All these sad souls lying still
beneath the rotting earth,

they need a kindly word,
their urns refreshed.

I make for the rusty tap beside
the gate, half fill the watering can.

Don't get yourself muddy, Mother cries.
But I need to visit my friend.

Little Lettice Legh departed 1610
in the ninth year of her age.

We would play Catch together
in the Great Hall, chasing in

and out of tapestry drapes,
our bare feet tap-tapping.

That day I caught her beside
the black stone fireplace,

grabbed her hair, slapped her cheek.
She slipped ... A widening pool

of red. I see her stretched out
on the couch, small hands

clasped across her chest,
her face pale as her linen nightgown.

I kneel, and tuck a bunch of buttercups
beneath the tilting headstone.

Flaneuse

I visited my grave last night
to lay flowers, then wafted
over the moonlit stones,
through the gate and into town.

I knew every bistro, every bar,
the boutiques where I bought clothes
to change my life. Now I needn't worry
about wearing heels that hurt.
Everything seems different now –
more colourful, more rich.

Pigeons on the balconies
have become flocks of flying angels,
cars are chariots, the buskers' raw
refrains are accompanied by harpsong,
and outside *The Frog and Fiddle* medieval alleys
teem with pedlars. Fops in powdered wigs
and satin pumps parade the Promenade,
the fountains shower liquid gold,
and on the High Street Woolworths
still stands selling bonbons.

NOTES

p.10 Lynx: Lynx is a constellation in the Northern hemisphere known in mythology as 'keeper of secrets'.

p.12 The Summons: Greek mythology tells how when Achilles was born his mother, the sea-goddess Thetis, held him over the River Styx by his foot to render him immortal, not realising his heel was covered by her hand and therefore vulnerable. He was later killed in battle.

p.13 Blodeuwedd: from a Welsh myth in the *Mabinogi* in which a lady made of flowers was turned into an owl because of her infidelity.

p.14 Sacrifice: a Hans Christian Anderson story about a mermaid who fell in love with a mortal Prince, and to her great cost took a witch's potion to change her tail into human limbs.

p.15 Salome: King Herod became besotted with the dancer, his stepdaughter, and granted her any wish if she would dance for him. She requested the head of John the Baptist.

p.34 Sophia: award-winning photograph taken by Nestor Diaz of his wife after her mastectomy, featured in the *National Portrait Gallery Photographic Exhibition 2012*.

p.35 Reverence: Andrew Bruce, an acclaimed artist/photographer, used road kill as inspiration for tender and mystical artwork. I was very moved when I attended an illustrated talk he gave about his beautiful, almost spiritual work, observing nature at the moment of death.

p.36 Stone Child, Bone Child: Mary Anning of Lyme Regis was an 18th century fossil-collector who acquired international fame as a palaeontologist. It was alleged that as a child she discovered remains of a dinosaur while digging on the beach.

p.40 1926: the year an English aristocrat, the Honourable Violet Albina Gibson, made an unsuccessful attempt to shoot Fascist leader, Benito Mussolini, with whom she was obsessed, as he was addressing his followers in Rome's piazza.

p.41 I Knitted You a Halo: an 80-year-old Spanish woman took it upon herself to restore a damaged fresco of Christ's face by 19th century artist, Elias Garcia Martinez, in the small Church of Sanctuario de Misericordia, Borja. Her calamitous work was dubbed *Ecco Mono – Behold the Monkey*, and became a tourist attraction.

Indigo Dreams Publishing Ltd
24, Forest Houses
Cookworthy Moor
Halwill
Beaworthy
Devon
EX21 5UU
www.indigodreams.co.uk